Fantastic Homes for Flying Creatures

I0880327

by Joanne Mattern

RED CHAIR PRESS
Egremont, Massachusetts

RED CHAIR PRESS
BOOKS FOR YOUNG READERS

Wildlife Rescue is produced and published by Red Chair Press:
Red Chair Press LLC PO Box 333 South Egremont, MA 01258-0333
www.redchairpress.com

Publisher's Cataloging-In-Publication Data
Names: Mattern, Joanne, 1963- author.
Title: Fantastic homes for flying creatures / by Joanne Mattern.

Description: South Egremont, MA : Red Chair Press, [2022] | Series: Wildlife rescue | Interest age level: 007-010. | Includes index and suggested resources for further reading. | Summary: "This book shows the importance of bat houses, bird houses, and butterfly shelters and how building these simple structures can save the lives of endangered species. Readers will also explore the importance of butterfly gardens and how they provide food and shelter for some of Earth's most fragile and beautiful creatures"--Provided by publisher.

Identifiers: ISBN 9781643711904 (hardcover) | ISBN 9781643711942 (softcover) | ISBN 9781643711980 (ePDF) | ISBN 9781643712024 (ePub 3 S&L) | ISBN 9781643712062 (ePub 3 TR) | ISBN 9781643712109 (Kindle)

Subjects: LCSH: Wildlife habitat improvement--Juvenile literature. | Animals and civilization--Juvenile literature. | Birdhouses--Juvenile literature. | Birds--Conservation--Juvenile literature. | Butterflies--Conservation--Juvenile literature. | CYAC: Wildlife habitat improvement. | Animals and civilization. | Birdhouses. | Birds. | Butterflies.

Classification: LCC SK356.W54 M383 2022 (print) | LCC SK356.W54 (ebook) | DDC 333.95/416--dc23

LC record available at: https://lccn.loc.gov/2021945555

Photo credits: P. 1, 4, 6–16, 18, 19, 22–28: iStock; cover, p. 17, 24, 25: Shutterstock; p. 5: Benoit Henrion; p. 8: Jeff Dinardo; p. 19: Keith Garton; p. 20: Alonzo Adams; p. 21: Myriad Botanical Gardens

Printed in United States of America
0422 1P CGF22

Table of Contents

Home, Sweet Home

Every living thing needs a safe place to live. A home provides shelter from cold temperatures or bad weather. A home protects creatures from danger. It is a safe place to raise a family.

Animals find homes in many places. Some live underground. Others live in trees. Many live in caves, under rocks, or in trees.

When land is cleared for building houses and roads, the natural homes of many animals may be destroyed.

Creatures that fly need homes too. Birds and bats and butterflies live in trees or bushes. But sometimes these animals need help finding shelter. That's where people can help. People have built many special homes for flying creatures.

Why Birds Need Houses

You may have seen a small wooden box hanging from a tree or standing on a pole. People often build these houses for birds. If birds make their own nests, why do people need to build homes for them? There are several reasons why.

Birdhouses can be simple wooden boxes.

Birds may build their nests in trees or bushes.

Many birds have lost the places where they used to nest. People cut down trees to build new homes or roads. They pave over places that used to be wild. That can mean birds have to find a new place to live.

Bird houses are a safe place for birds to live. They can lay their eggs inside. Bird houses protect birds and eggs from **predators**.

The Story of the Bluebird

During the 1900s, the eastern bluebird lived all over the eastern United States. But in the 1960s, people destroyed the birds' **habitat** to build houses and businesses. Bluebirds also had trouble with another bird, called the house sparrow. Sparrows often drove bluebirds away from their nests. With no safe place to live, many bluebirds died.

Female eastern bluebird

Male eastern bluebird

Nesting boxes are a safe place for bluebirds to raise their young.

People wanted to save the bluebird. In 1970, it was named New York State's official bird. In 1982, a group called the New York State Bluebird Society asked people to build nesting boxes for bluebirds. Thousands of people put up boxes for bluebirds. By 2005, the bluebird population had increased by 70 percent.

The Perfect Home

Not all birds like the same kind of bird house. People often place bluebird houses in pairs, about ten feet apart. That way, house sparrows can have one box and bluebirds can have the other. Instead of chasing bluebirds away, the house sparrows are their neighbors.

Purple martins nest in big **flocks**. The perfect bird house for them includes lots of little boxes. These bird houses can be up to 18 feet off the ground. They are often found near fields and water. That's where purple martins like to live!

Purple martins live in large group houses similar to apartment buildings.

Butterfly Gardens

Butterflies are another flying creature that needs some help from people. These insects don't live in houses. They like gardens! Many communities have built butterfly gardens. These gardens are filled with plants that butterflies like. They fly among the flowers to eat and lay their eggs.

Many parks have butterfly gardens built in flower beds. Butterflies like to live near the flowers they enjoy.

Some towns have built shelters for butterflies and bees.

In some cities, butterflies and flowers live in warm **greenhouses**. Oklahoma City built a huge greenhouse in the city center for plants and butterflies. People can visit the Myriad **Botanical** Gardens to see pretty plants and beautiful butterflies.

Butterfly gardens can be great community centers. In 2020, a gardening club in Indiana built a butterfly garden at the public library. Now when people come to get books, they can walk around the garden too. The library even holds programs in the garden. Butterflies are welcome to attend!

You can visit a big greenhouse for plants and butterflies in Oklahoma City.

Boxes for Bats

Bats can use some help finding homes too. Many bats have gotten sick and died over the past 15 years. Others have lost their habitats. A bat box can provide a safe place for bats to live.

People all over the country have built bat houses. It is important that these houses don't get too hot or too cold. If the temperature is just right, hundreds of bats can make bat houses their home. The University of Florida in Gainesville has the largest number of bat houses in the United States.

FAST FACTS:

Bats really do sleep upside down.

About 1 of every 5 mammals on Earth is a bat.

Bats are important pollinators just like bees and butterflies.

Bat houses can be hung in tall trees or on tall poles.

There are hundreds of bat houses at the University of Florida.

Little brown bats eat a lot of mosquitoes.

Some parks have built bat houses on their land. **Rangers** in Chenango Valley State Park in New York wanted bats to leave buildings where people gathered. So, they built several bat boxes. It took some time, but the park's little brown bats moved into their new homes. Now the bats, the rangers, and the park guests are happy!

Good Neighbors

Birds, butterflies, and bats are good neighbors. Bats and birds eat harmful insects. Birds spread seeds. Butterflies help **pollinate** plants so new flowers can grow.

People who help animals are good neighbors too. They make the world's parks, gardens, and backyards good places for everyone to live.

Glossary

botanical: having to do with plants and plant life

flocks: large groups of birds

greenhouses: heated glass buildings where plants grow

habitat: the natural place where an animal lives

pollinate: to move pollen from one plant to another

predators: animals that hunt other animals for food

rangers: people who work in a forest or park

Learn More in the Library

Davidson, Lauren. *Butterflies for Kids: A Junior Scientist's Guide*. Rockridge Press, 2021.

Delano, Marfe. *Explore My World: Butterflies*. National Geographic Kids.

Mattern, Joanne. *What's So Scary About Bats?* Red Chair Press, 2022.

Index

About the Author

Joanne Mattern is the author of many books for children including the Core Content: ***Earth's Amazing Animals Series***. She loves writing about sports, all kinds of animals, and interesting people. Mattern lives in New York State with her family.